A COMMENTARY ON CHAPTER EIGHT OF *AMORIS LAETITIA*

A COMMENTARY ON CHAPTER EIGHT OF *AMORIS LAETITIA*

CARDINAL
FRANCESCO COCCOPALMERIO

Foreword by
CARDINAL BLASE CUPICH,
ARCHBISHOP OF CHICAGO

Paulist Press
New York / Mahwah, NJ

Cover image (background) by HorenkO/Shutterstock.com
Cover and book design by Lynn Else

Originally published in Italian by Libreria Editrice Vaticana as *Il Capitolo
Ottavo della Esortazione Apostolica Post Sinodale* Amoris Laetitia

Copyright © 2017 by Libreria Editrice Vaticana
English translation and foreword, copyright ©2017 by Paulist Press
Translated by Sean O'Neill

All rights reserved. No part of this publication may be reproduced, stored
in a retrieval system, or transmitted in any form or by any means, electronic,
mechanical, photocopying, recording, scanning, or otherwise, without
either the prior written permission of the Publisher, or authorization
through payment of the appropriate per-copy fee to the Copyright
Clearance Center, Inc., www.copyright.com. Requests to the Publisher for
permission should be addressed to the Permissions Department, Paulist
Press, permissions@paulistpress.com.

Library of Congress Control Number: 2017939639

ISBN 978-0-8091-5369-5 (paperback)

Published by Paulist Press
997 Macarthur Boulevard
Mahwah, New Jersey 07430

www.paulistpress.com

Printed and bound in the
United States of America

CONTENTS

FOREWORD

Cardinal Blase Cupich,
Archbishop of Chicago

Controversies about Church teachings have oftentimes provided new opportunities to retrieve certain truths that have become dormant, thereby resulting in sharper articulations of the faith. That is surely the case in this present moment, as some have raised questions about the apostolic exhortation, *Amoris Laetitia*, issued by Pope Francis, following the two synods on marriage and family life.

The disputes cover a full range of issues, from how this document views the role of personal conscience to whether or not it represents an authentic development of Church doctrine. Some have even gone so far as to challenge the magisterial authority of this document signed by the pope.

All of this has provoked a robust discussion by scholars familiar with Church history and our wider theological tradition and pastoral practice. For instance, Rocco Buttiglione offered us in his July 2016 *L'Osservatore Romano* article a lesson on the development of doctrine and what it means for popes to exercise their divinely granted Petrine power of loosening and binding in different ways and in different historical circumstances. Likewise, James Keenan, SJ, crafted a superb remedial tutorial on the traditional understanding of conscience in *America*, December 2016. Finally, in the March 2017 English edition of *Civiltà Cattolica*, Anthony Spadaro, SJ, interviewed Cardinal Christoph Schönborn about the fundamental issues of this magisterial document, offering us an authoritative interpretation.

Now comes Cardinal Francesco Coccopalmerio with his readers' guide to the eighth chapter of this post-synodal exhortation. He notes from the outset that this chapter is dense with themes not often in order. He writes not in any official way, nor in response to any group or person. His aim is simply to offer a careful analysis of chapter 8 to help readers "grasp its rich doctrinal and pastoral message."

He is forthright in establishing that this magisterial document fully complies with traditional Church teaching on marriage, but is also in conformity with accepted standards of a pastoral approach that is positive and constructive. His exegesis of the document's treatment of the subjective conditions of conscience and the role of pastoral discernment highlights the real-life circumstances people face, and the mitigating factors which must be taken into consideration.

His treatment of the distinct aspects of the ontology or the reality of a person's being is perhaps his greatest contribution to the ongoing discussion of *Amoris Laetitia*. There are elements of a person's being that are shared in common with all of humanity and understood in a general and abstract way. At the same time, there are unique elements of each individual "that in some way limit the person, especially in the ability to understand, to will and therefore to act." For this reason, when it comes to dealing with certain so-called irregular situations, what is required is a pastoral approach that takes into consideration both the general and the individual aspects of a person's life, that is, the full ontology of the person. This, he observes, "has always been and is, especially today, crucial for the life of the Church, especially for its pastoral activity."

We oftentimes hear a narrative that those working in the Roman Curia are pastorally insensitive and out of touch with the ordinary lives of people. Cardinal Coccopalmerio, an accomplished canon lawyer, who serves as the President of the Pontifical Council for Legislative Texts, belies that portrayal in this exquisite exegesis of chapter 8 of *Amoris Laetitia*. He wisely counsels us that instead of being fearful when controversies about the faith arise, the teaching Church should rather embrace them as opportunities to be the good scribe of the Kingdom who, Jesus tells us, is "like the head of a household who brings from his storeroom both the new and the old."

PREFACE

Significantly, the eighth chapter of the post-synodal apostolic exhortation *Amoris Laetitia* is entitled "Accompanying, Discerning and Integrating Weakness."

This part of the document is not very large, composed of only twenty-two sections, 291 to 312, but it is very dense and therefore presents greater difficulties for analysis and understanding. To this, we may add that it has a certain inorganic quality, that is, it has a succession of themes that are not always in order.

Because of its content and its form, this chapter has been treated either with a certain disfavor or at least with some reserve. For this reason, it has been set aside, in a way, and not examined much, and therefore has been subjected to less careful and analytical exegesis.

The purpose of these pages, therefore, would be to take into detailed consideration the important text of chapter 8, in order to try to grasp its rich doctrinal and pastoral message.

I believe, however, that it will prove useful to offer here not a theoretical reflection on the text of the exhortation, so much as a reading of the text itself, which will enable us, on the one hand, to carry out a theoretical reflection on the various points in the document and, on the other, to familiarize ourselves with it in a direct way, and therefore savor the text of the document itself in the original.

The reading of these texts will, therefore, be a guided reading. However, I will not follow the numerical order of the paragraphs of chapter 8, but the succession of topics outlined below. By taking the individual texts as they appear in the logic of the arguments, it may be easier then to read them and understand them in numerical order.

With this in mind, it seems to me useful to identify and present six arguments:

1. An explanation of the Church's doctrine regarding marriage and the family;
2. The pastoral attitude of the Church toward people who find themselves in irregular situations;
3. The subjective conditions, or conditions of conscience, of different people in various irregular situations and the associated problem of admission to the sacraments of reconciliation and the Eucharist;
4. The problem of the relationship between doctrine and the rule in general, and individuals in particular;
5. Integration, that is, participation in the life of the Church and also in the ministry of the Church by people who find themselves in irregular situations.
6. Pope Francis's hermeneutic of the person.

1

AN EXPLANATION OF THE CHURCH'S DOCTRINE REGARDING MARRIAGE AND THE FAMILY

1.1. I think this is presented in a complete and clear way in the following text, where we read:

> Christian marriage, as a reflection of the union between Christ and his Church, is fully realized in the union between a man and a woman who give themselves to each other in a free, faithful and exclusive love, who belong to each other until death and are open to the transmission of life, and are consecrated by the sacrament, which grants them the grace to become a domestic church and a leaven of new life for society. Some forms of union radically contradict this ideal, while others realize it in at least a partial and analogous way. The Synod Fathers stated that the Church does not disregard the constructive elements in those situations which do not yet or no longer correspond to her teaching on marriage.[1] (#292)

It is evident that the quoted text contains with absolute clarity all the elements of the doctrine on marriage in full compliance with and fidelity to the traditional teaching of the Church.

In particular, we can highlight the affirmation of indissolubility, contained in the effective expression: "who belong to each other until death."

And then we also see a validation of this doctrine in the words: "Some forms of union radically contradict this ideal, while others realize it in at least a partial and analogous way."

The last part of the text introduces what we will say in the next point of our reading (see 2.2).

However, we should note that although the above text is based on the two citations, it is a new text presented for the first time in the exhortation.

1.2. The presentation of the doctrine of marriage and the family is followed up by a pastoral concern regarding its understanding by many young people. The exhortation says this:

> On the other hand, it is a source of concern that many young people today distrust marriage and live together, putting off indefinitely the commitment of marriage, while yet others break a commitment already made and immediately assume a new one. "As members of the Church, they too need pastoral care that is merciful and helpful."[2] (#293)

NOTES

1. *Relatio Synodi* 2014, 41–43; *Relatio Finalis* 2015, 70.
2. *Relatio Synodi* 2014, 26.

2

THE PASTORAL ATTITUDE OF THE CHURCH TOWARD PEOPLE WHO FIND THEMSELVES IN IRREGULAR SITUATIONS

We can say that the exhortation offers two points of view: the repeated affirmation of the firm resolve to remain faithful to the Church's teaching on marriage and the family; and the view of the Church, of pastors, and the faithful toward irregular partnerships, particularly civil marriages and de facto unions.

2.1. The repeated affirmation of the firm resolve to remain faithful to the Church's teaching on marriage and the family is shown by the following passages, where we read:

> ...a new union arising from a recent divorce, with all the suffering and confusion which this entails for children and entire families, or the case of someone who has consistently failed in his obligations to the family. It must remain clear that this is not the ideal which the Gospel proposes for marriage and the family. (#298)

> "...Given that gradualness is not in the law itself,[1] this discernment can never prescind from the Gospel demands of truth and charity, as proposed by the Church. For this discernment to happen, the following conditions must necessarily be present: humility, discretion and love for the Church and her teaching, in a sincere search for God's will and a desire to make a more perfect response to it."[2] These attitudes are essential for avoiding the grave danger of misunderstandings, such as the notion that any priest can quickly grant "exceptions," or

that some people can obtain sacramental privileges in exchange for favors. When a responsible and tactful person, who does not presume to put his or her own desires ahead of the common good of the Church, meets with a pastor capable of acknowledging the seriousness of the matter before him, there can be no risk that a specific discernment may lead people to think that the Church maintains a double standard. (#300)

For an adequate understanding of the possibility and need of special discernment in certain "irregular" situations, one thing must always be taken into account, lest anyone think that the demands of the Gospel are in any way being compromised. (#301)

In order to avoid all misunderstanding, I would point out that in no way must the Church desist from proposing the full ideal of marriage, God's plan in all its grandeur....A lukewarm attitude, any kind of relativism, or an undue reticence in proposing that ideal, would be a lack of fidelity to the Gospel and also of love on the part of the Church for young people themselves. To show understanding in the face of exceptional situations never implies dimming the light of the fuller ideal, or proposing less than what Jesus offers to the human being. (#307)

We can reread and then highlight some expressions that mean to affirm the full intention to be faithful to the traditional doctrine of the Church: "This discernment can never prescind from the Gospel demands of truth and charity, as proposed by the Church...there can be no risk that a specific discernment may lead people to think that the Church maintains a double standard" (#300); "lest anyone think that the demands of the Gospel are in any way being compromised" (#301); "in no way must the Church desist from proposing the full ideal of marriage, God's plan...any kind of relativism, or an undue reticence in proposing that ideal, would be a lack of fidelity to the Gospel...dimming the light of the fuller ideal, or proposing less than what Jesus offers..." (#307).

These expressions speak for themselves.

2.2. The view of the Church, of pastors, and the faithful toward irregular partnerships, particularly civil marriages and de facto unions.

Here there are a few texts we may read:

> The Fathers also considered the specific situation of a merely civil marriage or, with due distinction, even simple cohabitation, noting that "when such unions attain a particular stability, legally recognized, are characterized by deep affection and responsibility for their offspring, and demonstrate an ability to overcome trials, they can provide occasions for pastoral care with a view to the eventual celebration of the sacrament of marriage."[3] ...For the Church's pastors are not only responsible for promoting Christian marriage, but also the "pastoral discernment of the situations of a great many who no longer live this reality. Entering into pastoral dialogue with these persons is needed to distinguish elements in their lives that can lead to a greater openness to the Gospel of marriage in its

fullness."[4] In this pastoral discernment, there is a need "to identify elements that can foster evangelization and human and spiritual growth."[5] (#293)

"The choice of a civil marriage or, in many cases, of simple cohabitation, is often not motivated by prejudice or resistance to a sacramental union, but by cultural or contingent situations."[6] In such cases, respect can also be shown for those signs of love which in some way reflect God's own love (ibid.). "...Simply to live together is often a choice based on a general attitude opposed to anything institutional or definitive; it can also be done while awaiting more security in life (a steady job and steady income). In some countries, de facto unions are very numerous, not only because of a rejection of values concerning the family and matrimony, but primarily because celebrating a marriage is considered too expensive in the social circumstances. As a result, material poverty drives people into de facto unions."[7] ...Whatever the case, "all these situations require a constructive response seeking to transform them into opportunities that can lead to the full reality of marriage and family in conformity with the Gospel. These couples need to be welcomed and guided patiently and discreetly."[8] That is how Jesus treated the Samaritan woman (cf. John 4:1–26): he addressed her desire for true love, in order to free her from the darkness in her life and to bring her to the full joy of the Gospel. (#294)

As for the way of dealing with different "irregular" situations, the Synod Fathers reached a general consensus, which I support: "In considering a pastoral approach towards people who have contracted a civil marriage, who are divorced and remarried, or simply living together, the Church has the responsibility of helping them understand the divine pedagogy of grace in their lives and offering them assistance so they can reach the fullness of God's plan for them,"[9] something which is always possible by the power of the Holy Spirit. (#297)

It seems to me that the passages quoted contain a valuable message that is exquisitely pastoral. And, indeed, when dealing with irregular unions, such as civil marriages and even de facto unions, pastors must approach them in a positive and constructive way, which I think means having three important attitudes.

The first is to recognize, objectively, clearly and without preconceptions or hasty judgments, the reason that has led some believers to choose, not canonical marriage, but rather other forms of cohabitation: the reason for this is not always, or not frequently, a denial of the value of canonical marriage, but rather some contingency, such as lack of work and therefore of secure income.

The second attitude of pastors of souls must be to refrain from an immediate condemnation of irregular unions and to recognize that in many of them there are positive elements, such as stability, which can even be guaranteed by a public bond, a real affection toward the partner and toward the children, and a commitment to society or the Church.

A third attitude suggested by the texts is certainly one of dialogue with these couples, which means that the pastors of souls must not simply be satisfied with the irregular situation, but must strive to make the faithful who are in that situation reflect on the possibility, indeed on beauty and the opportunity, of realizing the celebration of a marriage in its fullness, before the Church.

NOTES

1. Cf. *Familiaris Consortio*, 34.
2. *Relatio Finalis* 2015, 85.
3. *Relatio Synodi* 2014, 27.
4. Ibid., 41.
5. Ibid.
6. *Relatio Finalis* 2015, 71.
7. *Relatio Synodi* 2014, 42.
8. Ibid., 43.
9. *Relatio Synodi* 2014, 25.

3

THE SUBJECTIVE
CONDITIONS,
OR CONDITIONS OF
CONSCIENCE,
OF DIFFERENT PEOPLE
IN VARIOUS IRREGULAR
SITUATIONS AND
THE ASSOCIATED PROBLEM
OF ADMISSION TO THE
SACRAMENTS OF
RECONCILIATION AND
THE EUCHARIST

This is the hardest part to understand precisely. There are a few aspects to consider.

3.1. I would begin with a text that seems to me foundational for the other statements:

> The Church possesses a solid body of reflection concerning mitigating factors and situations. Hence it can no longer simply be said that all those in any "irregular" situation are living in a state of mortal sin and are deprived of sanctifying grace. (#301)

By using the expression: "all those in any 'irregular' situation," the text just quoted aims to refer to all those who are married only civilly or living with a de facto union or tied to a previous canonical marriage. It is possible that all these faithful may not be living "in a state of mortal sin," and are not "deprived of sanctifying grace."

3.2. But what are the reasons for this moral judgment? It is very interesting to read the rest of the text just quoted above:

> More is involved here than mere ignorance of the rule. A subject may know full well the rule, yet have great difficulty in understanding "its inherent values,"[1] or be in a concrete situation which does not allow him or her to act differently and decide otherwise without further sin. As the Synod Fathers put it, "factors may exist which limit the ability to make a decision."[2] Saint Thomas Aquinas himself

15

recognized that someone may possess grace and charity, yet not be able to exercise any one of the virtues well;[3] in other words, although someone may possess all the infused moral virtues, he does not clearly manifest the existence of one of them, because the outward practice of that virtue is rendered difficult: "Certain saints are said not to possess certain virtues, in so far as they experience difficulty in the acts of those virtues, even though they have the habits of all the virtues."[4] (#301)

It seems to me that the quoted text contains three reasons that would exempt the person from being in a condition of mortal sin:

a. "a possible ignorance of the rule" and therefore lack of culpability in the case of infringement of that rule;

b. "great difficulty in understanding the inherent values in the moral rule." Therefore, knowledge of the rule but at the same time an inability to believe it to be good. We can easily see then that this inability to recognize that the rule is good, is in fact equivalent to lack of knowledge of the rule. And, therefore, lack of culpability in the case of infringement of that rule;

c. "a concrete situation which does not allow him or her to act differently and decide otherwise without further sin," "factors may exist which limit the ability to make a decision." In this case, there is knowledge of the rule and of its goodness, but an inability to act as the rule dictates without getting into further sin.

3.3. The first and second reasons require attention and discernment. Pastoral activity must ensure that the consciences of the faithful are formed by knowledge of the rule.

The third of the three reasons is the most problematic. How are we to understand it exactly? Here another text comes to our aid:

> ...a second union consolidated over time, with new children, proven fidelity, generous self giving, Christian commitment, a consciousness of its irregularity and of the great difficulty of going back without feeling in conscience that one would fall into new sins. The Church acknowledges situations "where, for serious reasons, such as the children's upbringing, a man and woman cannot satisfy the obligation to separate."[5] (#298)

In this text, we would like to highlight these expressions: (a) "second union consolidated over time"; (b) "with new children"; (c) "proven fidelity, generous self giving, Christian commitment"; (d) "consciousness of its irregularity"; (e) "great difficulty of going back without feeling in conscience that one would fall into new sins"; (f) "serious reasons, such as the children's upbringing"; (g) "cannot satisfy the obligation to separate."

We can easily see that the text of #298 contains expressions parallel to those of the text we examined previously, that is, from #301.

Let's look at the parallel expressions of the two passages cited:

> "concrete situation which does not allow him or her to act differently and decide otherwise…" and "factors may exist which limit the ability to make a decision." (#301)

> "great difficulty of going back without feeling in conscience that one would fall into new sins" and "a man and woman cannot satisfy the obligation to separate." (#298)

In order to clarify our thinking, we can further break down the above two parallel expressions into three segments in turn, which are, of course, parallel:

a. "to act differently" and "decide otherwise" (#301)—"go back" (#298). The meaning of the first expression is easily understood: to abandon the irregular situation. The meaning of "go back" is clearly indicated by the expression in the text itself: "satisfy the obligation to separate," so we have the same meaning: to abandon the irregular situation;

b. "without further sin" (#301)—"without feeling in conscience that one would fall into new sins" (#298). The meaning, therefore, is clear: abandoning the irregular situation would entail the commission of a new sin;

c. "a concrete situation which does not allow…" and "factors…which limit the ability to make a decision" (#301)—"for serious reasons...a man and woman cannot" (#298). These expressions aim to explain why abandoning the irregular situation would entail the commission of a new sin: the reason is that there are "concrete situations," "factors," and "reasons" that do not allow it.

The concrete situations, factors, and reasons that we are referring to, are those that we have outlined in a, b, and c. For this reason, those who are in the irregular situation which, however, is "consolidated over time," has "new children," is marked by "proven fidelity, generous self giving, Christian commitment," cannot abandon such a situation, cannot "satisfy the obligation to separate."

However, we may ask ourselves why. And the only possible reason seems to be the following: in the cases we have mentioned, abandoning the irregular situation would harm other people who are themselves innocent, namely the partner and the children, especially the latter, who could be at a delicate age or be in problematic circumstances and therefore be particularly in need of paternal and maternal care.

But there is another element contained here in the text and it is crucial for understanding this delicate problem correctly. It is contained in this expression: "consciousness of its irregularity."

The text, therefore, states that the people in question are conscious of the "irregularity"; they are, in other words, conscious of the sinful condition.

The text, however, does not claim that the aforesaid persons intend to change their irregular status. It does not claim this explicitly, but it certainly presupposes it implicitly:

in fact, thereafter, it speaks about the "great difficulty of going back without feeling in conscience that one would fall into new sins" and "cannot satisfy the obligation to separate." This clearly means that the people in question have considered the problem of changing and thus they intend to, or at least desire to, change their situation.

To better illustrate what has been said until now, let us turn to a tangible case, that is, the case of a woman who has gone to live with a man who was canonically married but was abandoned by his wife and left with three young children. However, this woman has saved the man from a state of deep despair, and probably from the temptation to commit suicide; he has brought up the three children not without considerable sacrifice; their union then lasts for ten years; a new child is born. The woman in question is fully aware of being in an irregular situation. She would sincerely like to change their living situation, but, evidently, cannot. In fact, if she left the union, the man would return to his former state, and the children would remain without a mother. Leaving the union would mean, therefore, not fulfilling important duties toward persons who are in themselves innocent. It is therefore evident that this could not take place "without further sin."

3.4. However, this raises the usual objection: properly speaking, the cohabitants above should live "as brother and sister," in other words, should abstain completely from sexual relations.

In this regard, we can reread the well-known text from *Familiaris Consortio*, 84, which runs as follows:

> Reconciliation in the sacrament of Penance which would open the way to the Eucharist, can only be granted to those who, repenting of having broken

the sign of the Covenant and of fidelity to Christ, are sincerely ready to undertake a way of life that is no longer in contradiction to the indissolubility of marriage. This means, in practice, that when, for serious reasons, such as for example the children's upbringing, a man and a woman cannot satisfy the obligation to separate, they "take on themselves the duty to live in complete continence, that is, by abstinence from the acts proper to married couples."[6]

At this point let us return to reading *Amoris Laetitia* and we can examine footnote 329, which proves to be especially interesting. Let us begin by looking at what this text says:

In such situations, many people, knowing and accepting the possibility of living "as brothers and sisters" which the Church offers them, point out that if certain expressions of intimacy are lacking, "it often happens that faithfulness is endangered and the good of the children suffers."[7] (#298, footnote 329)

The footnote in *Amoris Laetitia* therefore refers to *Gaudium et Spes*, 51, and quotes some expressions from it, which, however, it would be well to read in full:

This council realizes that certain modern conditions often keep couples from arranging their married lives harmoniously, and that they find themselves in circumstances where at least temporarily the size of their families should not be increased. As a result, the faithful exercise of love and the full intimacy of their lives is hard to maintain. But where the intimacy of married life is broken off, its faithfulness can sometimes be imperiled and its quality of fruitfulness ruined, for then the upbringing of the children and the courage to accept new ones are both endangered.

It is important to ask what exactly is meant by the expression used by the Council: "The intimacy of married life" (in the original Latin: *intima vita coniugalis*). This undoubtedly means the fulfillment of conjugal acts. Over and above the meaning of these words, we are also led to this interpretation by what is also stated above: "at least temporarily the size of their families should not be increased."

At this point, the text states: "...where the intimacy of married life is broken off (Latin: *abrumpitur*)," and thus the fulfillment of conjugal acts ceases, "its faithfulness can sometimes be imperiled and its quality of fruitfulness ruined, for then the upbringing of the children and the courage to accept new ones are both endangered."

It is natural to observe that the opportunity to not refrain from the fulfillment of conjugal acts, in order to avoid the situation where "faithfulness...and the upbringing of the children...are...endangered," is an indication given by the Council for marital situations, in other words legitimate unions, while the apostolic exhortation applies it to cases of marriages that are, at least objectively, irregular. I believe, however, that this difference is not relevant to the correctness of the aforementioned application.

In the light of these texts, it seems to me that we can say that:

a. where the commitment to live "as brother and sister" turns out to be possible without any difficulty for the couple's relationship, the partners accept it willingly;

b. however, if this commitment is deemed to be difficult, the two partners seem not to be obligated per se, because they correspond to the case spoken of in #301 where it says clearly that they can find themselves "in a concrete situation which does not allow him or her to act differently and decide otherwise without further sin."

3.5. Note carefully that in the above hypothetical case the impossibility of acting differently, that is, of leaving the union, is determined by objective evidence (partner, children).

But there is another reason why it becomes impossible, or at least very difficult to do otherwise. Let us look at a couple of passages:

The Church possesses a solid body of reflection concerning mitigating factors and situations. (#301)

The *Catechism of the Catholic Church* clearly mentions these factors: "imputability and responsibility for an action can be diminished or even nullified by ignorance, inadvertence, duress, fear, habit, inordinate attachments, and other psychological or social factors."[8] In another paragraph, the Catechism refers once again to circumstances which mitigate moral responsibility, and mentions at length "affective immaturity, force of acquired habit, conditions of anxiety or other psychological or social factors that lessen or even extenuate moral culpability."[9] For this reason, a negative judgment about an objective situation does not imply a judgment about the imputability or culpability of the person involved.[10] On the basis of these convictions, I consider very fitting what many Synod Fathers wanted to affirm: "Under certain circumstances people find it very difficult to act differently. Therefore, while upholding a general rule, it is necessary to recognize that responsibility with respect to certain actions or decisions is not the same in all cases. Pastoral discernment, while taking into account a person's properly formed conscience, must take responsibility for these situations. Even the consequences of actions taken are not necessarily the same in all cases."[11] (302)

In the cases described above, the impossibility of doing otherwise, that is, discontinuing the negative situation, is determined not by objective reasons as in the previous case, but by subjective reasons, that is, by behavioral conditioning. But the result seems to be the same.

3.6. Then note the conclusion of *Amoris Laetitia*, albeit in a text that is rather different from the previous one:

Because of forms of conditioning and mitigating factors, it is possible that in an objective situation of sin—which may not be subjectively culpable, or fully such—a person can be living in God's grace, can love and can also grow in the life of grace and charity, while receiving the Church's help to this end. (#305)

This text is consonant, almost literally, with #301, which we have already quoted above: "Hence it can no longer simply be said that all those in any 'irregular' situation are living in a state of mortal sin and are deprived of sanctifying grace."

That said, the text refers to footnote 351, which is interesting and which we need to read carefully:

> In certain cases, this can include the help of the sacraments. Hence, "I want to remind priests that the confessional must not be a torture chamber, but rather an encounter with the Lord's mercy" (Apostolic Exhortation *Evangelii Gaudium* [November 24, 2013], 44: AAS 105 [2013], 1038). I would also point out that the Eucharist "is not a prize for the perfect, but a powerful medicine and nourishment for the weak." (ibid., 47: 1039)

3.7. The Church, therefore, could allow access to Penance and the Eucharist, for the faithful who find themselves in an irregular union, which, however, requires two essential conditions: they desire to change the situation, but cannot act on their desire.

Clearly, the essential conditions above must be carefully and authoritatively discerned by the ecclesial authority. The well-known principle is very true and, in fact, very apt, especially on these occasions: *Nemo judex in causa propria.*

The ecclesial authority will, at least normally, be the pastor, who knows the people directly, and for this reason he can make a proper judgment in these delicate situations.

However, it could be necessary, or at least very useful, to have a service of the Curia, in which the diocesan Ordinary, in a similar way to what is provided for in difficult marriage cases, offers appropriate counseling or even specific authorization in these cases regarding admission to the sacraments of reconciliation and the Eucharist.

However, there is an obstacle to overcome, namely the scandal that this concession would be to the community. By using the word *scandal*, we express the following erroneous judgment: because the Church admits to the sacraments some of the Christian faithful who are in an irregular union, this means that the union is regular and that marriage is either not necessary or not indissoluble.

It is therefore essential to avoid the aforesaid scandal. And this is achieved by instructing the faithful and in a practical way offering to them the following yardstick: when the faithful who live in irregular situations are allowed access to the Eucharistic table, this means that the faithful themselves, in the judgment of the Church which knows their situation, confirms that the two conditions, which must always be considered essential, have been satisfied: the desire to change and the inability to do so.

In any case, it is obvious that the competent ecclesiastical authorities, I would say the Episcopal Conferences, should promptly issue some guidelines to instruct the faithful and their pastors in this delicate matter.

3.8. At this point, having carefully considered, without preconceptions and—we hope—having faithfully analyzed, all the elements contained in the exhortation, we can evaluate theologically the possible admission of one of the faithful to the sacraments of reconciliation and the Eucharist.

I think we can assume, with a sure and clear conscience that, in this case, the doctrine is respected.

The doctrine of the indissolubility of marriage is respected in this case, because the faithful in this hypothetical case are not in legitimate unions, on the contrary, more precisely, we can certainly say that such a condition is objectively a grave sin.

The doctrine of genuine repentance, which involves the intention of changing their state of life as a necessary prerequisite for admission to the sacrament of Penance is respected in this case, so that the faithful in these hypothetical situations, on the one hand, are conscious, and have the conviction, of the state of objective sin in which they currently find themselves and, on the other, have the intention of changing their way of life, even if, at this time, they are not able to implement their resolution.

The doctrine of sanctifying grace as a prerequisite for being admitted to the sacrament of the Eucharist is also respected because the faithful in question, even if, at this time, they have not yet arrived at a real change in their state of life because of the impossibility of doing so, do, however, have the intention of implementing such a change.

And it is exactly this context, the theological factor, that permits absolution and access to the Eucharist, but always—we repeat—when an inability to quickly change the condition of sin is present.

So to whom can the Church absolutely not—because it would be a patent contradiction—grant reconciliation and the Eucharist? To the faithful who, knowing that they are in grave sin and being able to change, still, however, have no sincere intention of implementing that change. The exhortation refers to this in the following words:

Naturally, if someone flaunts an objective sin as if it were part of the Christian ideal, or wants to impose something other than what the Church teaches, he or she can in no way presume to teach or preach to others; this is a case of something which separates from the community (cf. Matt 18:17). Such a person needs to listen once more to the Gospel message and its call to conversion. (#297)

NOTES

1. John Paul II, Apostolic Exhortation *Familiaris Consortio* (November 22, 1981), 33: AAS 74 (1982), 121.

2. *Relatio Finalis* 2015, 51.

3. Cf. *Summa Theologiae* III, q. 65, a. 3, ad 2; *De Malo* q. 2, a. 2.

4. Ibid., ad 3.

5. *Familiaris Consortio*, 84.

6. John Paul II, *Homily at the Close of the Sixth Synod of Bishops*, 7 (Oct. 25, 1980): AAS 72 (1980), 1082.

7. Second Vatican Ecumenical Council, Pastoral Constitution on the Church in the Modern World *Gaudium et Spes*, 51.

8. CCC 1735.

9. Ibid., 2352. All of footnote 344 is doctrinally interesting:

Congregation for the Doctrine of the Faith, Declaration on Euthanasia *Iura et Bona* (May 5, 1980), II: AAS 72 (1980), 546; John Paul II, in his critique of the category of "fundamental option," recognized that "doubtless there can occur situations which are very complex and obscure from a psychological viewpoint, and which have an influence on the sinner's subjective culpability" (Apostolic Exhortation *Reconciliatio et Paenitentia* [December 2, 1984], 17: AAS 77 [1985], 223).

10. Cf. Pontifical Council for Legislative Texts, *Declaration Concerning the Admission to Holy Communion of Faithful Who are Divorced and Remarried* (June 24, 2000), 2.

11. *Relatio Finalis* 2015, 85.

4

THE PROBLEM OF THE RELATIONSHIP BETWEEN DOCTRINE AND THE RULE IN GENERAL, AND INDIVIDUALS IN PARTICULAR

What was stated in the previous chapter has its roots in a broader subject, in something marginal.

4.1. First let us look at some passages from the exhortation:

> It is reductive simply to consider whether or not an individual's actions correspond to a general law or rule, because that is not enough to discern and ensure full fidelity to God in the concrete life of a human being. I earnestly ask that we always recall a teaching of Saint Thomas Aquinas and learn to incorporate it in our pastoral discernment: "Although there is necessity in the general principles, the more we descend to matters of detail, the more frequently we encounter defects....In matters of action, truth or practical rectitude is not the same for all, as to matters of detail, but only as to the general principles; and where there is the same rectitude in matters of detail, it is not equally known to all....The principle will be found to fail, according as we descend further into detail."[1] It is true that general rules set forth a good which can never be disregarded or neglected, but in their formulation they cannot provide absolutely for all particular situations. At the same time, it must be said that, precisely for that reason, what is part of a practical discernment in particular circumstances cannot be elevated to the level of a rule. That would not only lead to an intolerable casuistry, but would

endanger the very values which must be preserved with special care. (#304)

Supporting this text, we must read footnote 348:

In another text, referring to the general knowledge of the rule and the particular knowledge of practical discernment, Saint Thomas states that "if only one of the two is present, it is preferable that it be the knowledge of the particular reality, which is closer to the act.": *Sententia Libri Ethicorum*, VI, 6 (ed. Leonina, t. XLVII, 354)

Let us continue reading the text:

For this reason, a pastor cannot feel that it is enough simply to apply moral laws to those living in "irregular" situations, as if they were stones to throw at people's lives. This would bespeak the closed heart of one used to hiding behind the Church's teachings, "sitting on the chair of Moses and judging at times with superiority and superficiality difficult cases and wounded families."[2] Along these same lines, the International Theological Commission has noted that "natural law could not be presented as an already established set of rules that impose themselves a priori on the moral subject; rather, it is a source of objective inspiration for the deeply personal process of making decisions."[3]

4.2. The problem of the relationship between the doctrine and the rule in their generality and individuals in particular is, however, fundamental, but it is complex and requires careful reflection. Here we must limit ourselves to a few annotations.

a. All that is required is an initial examination of a person's being, in order to immediately grasp that it has a double aspect.

On the one hand, everyone has common elements that constitute the reality of the person, these are the ontology of the person considered in its generality, that is, precisely, in the elements that are common to all people.

On the other hand, each person, while he or she possesses the common elements referred to above, has at the same time individual elements, which constitute the reality of the person, these are also the ontology of the person, considered, however, in its individuality, in its singularity, in its concreteness.

As we have said, each person, because of the common elements, is equal to any other person, but, because of the individual elements, is also different from any other person.

Observe carefully, therefore, that whether referring to the common elements or to the individual elements, we are speaking of the ontology of the person.

However, we can identify and distinguish between two types of ontology of the person.

The first kind is an ontology that is constituted by the common elements and only the common elements, and which therefore has the characteristic of being general and abstract.

The second kind is an ontology that is constituted by common elements together with the individual elements and therefore has the characteristic of being individual and concrete.

However there does not seem to be any doubt that, in speaking of the ontology of the person, it is necessary to refer not only to the common elements, but at the same time to the individual elements, for the simple and obvious reason that these elements too, if they do not constitute, nor can they constitute, the general and therefore abstract ontology of every person, do, however, constitute the individual and therefore concrete ontology of this person.

b. The above seems particularly interesting in the case of those elements that in some way limit the person, especially in the ability to understand, to will, and therefore to act.

In these cases, we are in the presence not only of a person but also of a person with the individual and limiting characteristic which consists in the inability to act normally.

Different passages in the exhortation deal with these elements that limit the person in his or her capacity to act, by using terms such as "conditioning" or "extenuating circumstances" and employing the image of "weakness." Let us examine a few of these passages.

Regarding conditioning and mitigating circumstances, we can reread the two passages quoted above in section 3.5.

Regarding the image of weakness, we note that it already appears in the title of chapter 8 and then recurs thereafter in various passages:

The Synod Fathers stated that, although the Church realizes that any breach of the marriage bond "is against the will of God," she is also "conscious of the frailty of many of her children."[4] "…The Church must accompany with attention and care the weakest of her children, who show signs of a wounded and troubled love…."[5] (#291)

The Synod addressed various situations of weakness or imperfection. (#296)

But I sincerely believe that Jesus wants a Church attentive to the goodness which the Holy Spirit sows in the midst of human weakness….The Church's pastors, in proposing to the faithful the full ideal of the Gospel and the Church's teaching, must also help them to treat the weak with compassion…. (#308)

c. To respect the ontology of the person has always been and is, especially today, crucial for the life of the Church, especially for its pastoral activity.

Pay close attention now that when I say: respect the ontology of the person, I refer to the two aspects of this ontology, to that of the common elements and that of the individual elements.

And, indeed, I think that the Church, while at other times seeming to give importance only to the first aspect, nowadays, by contrast, seems to give more and more of its pastoral attention also to the second aspect.

Perhaps such behavior had its starting point, or at least a significant increase (because nothing is really new in the

Church) with the Second Vatican Council and offers clear examples through the pastoral style of Pope Francis.

4.3. In considering the ontology of the person by also taking into account its individual elements and particularly those that in some way restrict the person in his or her ability to act normally, the exhortation, it seems to me, is led toward three important consequences: the so-called "law of gradualness"; the development of the potential good; and the fact that all those people who do not fulfill the law or comply with it only in part are not necessarily culpable and the consequent need to refrain from judging these people as being guilty and therefore in a condition of grave sin.

a.   The so-called "law of gradualness" occurs many times in the teachings of Pope Francis, in the proposals of the Synod of Bishops and in the exhortation *Amoris Laetitia*. Let us at least look at one of those passages:

Along these lines, Saint John Paul II proposed the so-called "law of gradualness" in the knowledge that the human being "knows, loves and accomplishes moral good by different stages of growth."[6] This is not a "gradualness of law" but rather a gradualness in the prudential exercise of free acts on the part of subjects who are not in a position to understand, appreciate, or fully carry out the objective demands of the law. For the law is itself a gift of God which points out the way, a gift for everyone without exception; it can be followed with the help of grace, even though each human being "advances gradually with the progressive integration of the gifts of God and the demands of God's definitive and absolute love in his or her entire personal and social life."[7] (#295)

The so-called "law of gradualness," therefore, presupposes that a person has an inability, or serious difficulty, in implementing the law, at least in its totality, in all its requirements, because of a condition of weakness.

To these faithful, pastors of souls, on the one hand, must indicate the ideal, that is, the law in its entirety, and in all its requirements, but, on the other hand, must also facilitate the healing of their weakness, that is, increase their ability to act, utilizing for this work the normal means of pastoral ministry, especially preaching and the sacraments.

Now we must distinguish another case where there remains the impossibility, or serious difficulty, of putting the law into practice.

And, in fact, the law is given for all people, and does not consider, nor could it, cases where there is an inability to act normally and thus observe the law, in which individual persons can find themselves, such as a state of illness.

We may recall that, using pastoral wisdom to provide for such conditions of incapacity, canon law has already supplied some remedies that are referred to in a comprehensive manner as *aequitas canonica* and provide for exemptions, dispensations, and *epikeia*.

However, in the case of the "law of gradualness," the impossibility or great difficulty of putting the law into practice is caused by an inability of the will because of a condition of weakness of the will.

At this point the exhortation arrives at two doctrinally and pastorally very relevant outcomes.

b. The first outcome is the development of the potential good. Let us look at some texts:

Recognizing the influence of such concrete factors, we can add that individual conscience needs to be better incorporated into the Church's praxis in certain situations which do not objectively embody our understanding of marriage. Naturally, every effort should be made to encourage the development of an enlightened conscience, formed and guided by the responsible and serious discernment of one's pastor, and to encourage an ever greater trust in God's grace. Yet conscience can do more than recognize that a given situation does not correspond objectively to the overall demands of the Gospel. It can also recognize with sincerity and honesty what for now is the most generous response which can be given to God, and come to see with a certain moral security that it is what God himself is asking amid the concrete complexity of one's limits, while yet not fully the objective ideal. In any event, let us recall that this discernment is dynamic; it must remain ever open to new stages of growth and to new decisions which can enable the ideal to be more fully realized. (#303)

Discernment must help to find possible ways of responding to God and growing in the midst of limits. By thinking that everything is black and white, we sometimes close off the way of grace and of growth, and discourage paths of sanctification which give glory to God. Let us remember that "a small step, in the midst of great human limitations, can be more pleasing to God than a life which appears outwardly in order, but moves through the day without confronting great difficulties."[8] The practical pastoral care of ministers and of communities must not fail to embrace this reality. (#305)

At the same time, from our awareness of the weight of mitigating circumstances—psychological, historical and even biological—it follows that "without detracting from the evangelical ideal, there is a need to accompany with mercy and patience the eventual stages of personal growth as these progressively appear," making room for "the Lord's mercy, which spurs us on to do our best."[9] ...a Church...a Mother who, while clearly expressing her objective teaching, "always does what good she can, even if in the process, her shoes get soiled by the mud of the street."[10] (#308)

The three texts just quoted are undoubtedly of great human and pastoral value. I think it is important to reread three particular expressions:

...what for now is the most generous response which can be given to God...is what God himself is asking amid the concrete complexity of one's limits. (#303)

...possible ways of responding to God and growing in the midst of limits..."a small step, in the midst of great human limitations, can be more pleasing to God." (#305)

...the eventual stages of personal growth..."the Lord's mercy, which spurs us on to do our best"...a Church...a Mother who..."always does what good she can..." (#308)

These expressions speak for themselves. They are, however, marked by great realism and great respect for the specific ontology of every person. We also note the statement that God himself requires only what is possible and, therefore, is pleased with what is possible. It is the same for the Church as Mother.

    c. The second outcome: the fact that all those people who do not fulfill the law or comply with it only in part are not necessarily culpable, and the consequent need to refrain from judging these people as being guilty and therefore in a condition of grave sin. Here we can reference a couple of texts:

It is reductive simply to consider whether or not an individual's actions correspond to a general law or rule, because that is not enough to discern and ensure full fidelity to God in the concrete life of a human being. (#304)

The Church's pastors, in proposing to the faithful the full ideal of the Gospel and the Church's teaching, must also help them to treat the weak with compassion, avoiding aggravation or unduly harsh or hasty judgments. The Gospel itself tells us not to judge or condemn (cf. Matt 7:1; Luke 6:37). Jesus "expects us to stop looking for those personal or communal niches which shelter us from the maelstrom of human misfortune, and instead to enter into the reality of other people's lives and to know the power of tenderness. Whenever we do so, our lives become wonderfully complicated."[11] (#308)

We can also reread the valuable text in #305 already quoted above (cf. 4.1).

I would say that all this fully supports what we have stated above regarding the person and the fact that acting morally may be made impossible by real-life conditions, such as that exemplified by the woman who has been cohabiting for years, who is aware of the illegitimacy of her union, is genuinely eager to put the end to it, however, is unable, at least at present, to put her resolution into practice.

NOTES

1. *Summa Theologiae* I–II, q. 94, art. 4.

2. *Address for the Conclusion of the Fourteenth Ordinary General Assembly of the Synod of Bishops* (October 24, 2015): *L'Osservatore Romano* (October 26–27, 2015), 13.

3. International Theological Commission, *In Search of a Universal Ethic: A New Look at Natural Law* (2009), 59.

4. *Relatio Synodi* 2014, 24.

5. Ibid., 28.

6. Apostolic Exhortation *Familiaris Consortio* (November 22, 1981), 34: AAS 74 (1982), 123.

7. Ibid., 9.

8. Apostolic Exhortation *Evangelii Gaudium* (November 2013), 44: AAS 105 (2013), 1038–1039.

9. Ibid., 44.

10. Ibid., 45.

11. Ibid., 270.

5

INTEGRATION, THAT
IS, PARTICIPATION
IN THE LIFE OF THE
CHURCH AND ALSO IN
THE MINISTRY OF THE
CHURCH BY PEOPLE
WHO FIND THEMSELVES
IN IRREGULAR
SITUATIONS

A further aspect seems to emerge from chapter 8 as indicated in its title.

First, the exhortation offers us some general statements about the need for integration. Here are two passages:

> The Synod addressed various situations of weakness or imperfection. Here I would like to reiterate something I sought to make clear to the whole Church, lest we take the wrong path: "There are two ways of thinking which recur throughout the Church's history: casting off and reinstating. The Church's way, from the time of the Council of Jerusalem, has always been the way of Jesus, the way of mercy and reinstatement....The way of the Church is not to condemn anyone for ever; it is to pour out the balm of God's mercy on all those who ask for it with a sincere heart....For true charity is always unmerited, unconditional and gratuitous."[1] Consequently, there is a need "to avoid judgments which do not take into account the complexity of various situations" and "to be attentive, by necessity, to how people experience distress because of their condition."[2] (#296)

> It is a matter of reaching out to everyone, of needing to help each person find his or her proper way of participating in the ecclesial community and thus to experience being touched by an "unmerited, unconditional and gratuitous" mercy. No one

can be condemned for ever, because that is not the logic of the Gospel! Here I am not speaking only of the divorced and re-married, but of everyone, in whatever situation they find themselves. Naturally, if someone flaunts an objective sin as if it were part of the Christian ideal, or wants to impose something other than what the Church teaches, he or she can in no way presume to teach or preach to others; this is a case of something which separates from the community (cf. Matt 18:17). Such a person needs to listen once more to the Gospel message and its call to conversion. Yet even for that person there can be some way of taking part in the life of community, whether in social service, prayer meetings or another way that his or her own initiative, together with the discernment of the parish priest, may suggest. (#297)

5.2. At this point, it seems to me that the exhortation indicates two forms of integration into the life of the Church: the first would consist in comprehensive ministry and the second in the exercise of fraternal charity.

Regarding comprehensive ministry, we have the following:

I am in agreement with the many Synod Fathers who observed that "the baptized who are divorced and civilly remarried need to be more fully integrated into Christian communities in the variety of ways possible, while avoiding any occasion of scandal. The logic of integration is the key to their pastoral care, a care which would allow them not only to realize that they belong to the Church as the body of Christ, but also to know that they can have a joyful and fruitful experience in it. They are baptized; they are brothers and sisters; the Holy Spirit pours into their hearts gifts and talents for the good of all. Their participation can be expressed in different ecclesial services, which necessarily requires discerning which of the various forms of exclusion currently practiced in the liturgical, pastoral, educational and institutional framework, can be surmounted. Such persons need to feel not as excommunicated members of the Church, but instead as living members, able to live and grow in the Church and experience her as a mother who welcomes them always, who takes care of them with affection and encourages them along the path of life and the Gospel. This integration is also needed in the care and Christian upbringing of their children, who ought to be considered most important."[3] (#299)

Regarding the exercise of fraternal charity, we can read the following:

In every situation, when dealing with those who have difficulties in living God's law to the full, the invitation to pursue the *via caritatis* must be clearly heard. Fraternal charity is the first law of Christians (cf. John 15:12; Gal 5:14). Let us not forget the reassuring words of Scripture: "Maintain constant love for one another, for love covers a multitude of sins" (1 Pet 4:8); "Atone for your sins with righteousness, and your iniquities with mercy to the oppressed, so that your prosperity may be prolonged" (Dan 4:27); "As water extinguishes a blazing fire, so almsgiving atones for sins" (Sir 3:30). This is also what Saint Augustine teaches: "Just as, at the threat of a fire, we would run for water to extinguish it...so too, if the flame of sin rises from our chaff and we are troubled, if the chance to perform a work of mercy is offered us, let us rejoice in it, as if it were a fountain offered us to extinguish the blaze."[4] (#306)

NOTES

1. *Homily at Mass Celebrated with the New Cardinals* (February 15, 2015): AAS 107 (2015), 257.

2. *Relatio Finalis* 2015, 51.

3. Ibid., 84.

4. *De Catechizandis Rudibus*, I, 14, 22: PL 40, 327; cf. Apostolic Exhortation *Evangelii Gaudium* (November 24, 2013), 194: AAS 105 (2013), 1101.

6

POPE FRANCIS'S
HERMENEUTIC OF
THE PERSON

It seems to me that yet again Pope Francis's hermeneutic of the person is being affirmed, this time ensuring that no one is excluded. This is because the person, and therefore every person in whatever condition they find themselves, has value in and of themselves, despite the elements of moral negativity that they may have. The Pope reiterates nonexclusion on many occasions and in many forms.

What does the hermeneutic of the person mean? Hermeneutics—as we know—is a tool for knowledge and, therefore, a way of thinking, of evaluating reality, and of interpreting the world. Pope Francis uses the person as a means of interpretation.

In other words, Pope Francis evaluates reality through the person, or rather, he puts the person first and thus evaluates reality. What matters is the person, the rest comes as a logical consequence.

And the person has value in itself, regardless of the reason for its structural characteristics or its moral condition.

A person can be beautiful or not beautiful, intelligent or unintelligent, educated or ignorant, young or old; these structural characteristics are irrelevant. Every person, in fact, has value in themselves, and is therefore important and lovable.

A person can be good or not, and even this, especially this, does not matter: every person, even one who is not good, has intrinsic value, and is therefore important and lovable.

From here we derive a principle which is a fundamental element in the life of Pope Francis: his opposition to all ways in which people are marginalized. He repeats this continuously. No person should be excluded.

The reference to Jesus is evident, especially in two parables in the Gospel of Luke: the parable of the shepherd who goes in search of the hundredth sheep that is lost (this poor one is not excluded) (see Luke 15:1–7) and the parable of the prodigal son (and there is no exclusion for him either) (see Luke 15:11–32).

The love of Jesus and the Father, which is the same as that of the shepherd and of the Father in the two parables, is such that they highly value not only individuals who do some good—note well—but especially those who are in most need of their care. They cannot do without any of them, and they feel revitalized when they find the lost sheep or when the son returns.

The spirit and style of Pope Francis, it seems to me, is like this—in other words, and to return to our initial subject—this is his hermeneutic of the person.

Certainly, by practicing this love, Pope Francis incurs the well-known risks of the shepherd of the lost sheep and the father of the prodigal son. The shepherd may be injured, the father may suffer, even things that are more painful perhaps than a wound—the protests of the eldest son, who does not understand why the father will accept the prodigal son with love.

Beyond this very lively image, Pope Francis has also experienced and still experiences wounds and misunderstandings because of his hermeneutic of the person. In other words, if the shepherd seeks for the lost sheep, that is, the person of the sinner, if the father takes back the son, that is, the person who has sinned, if the Pope accepts the sinner, if the Pope does not marginalize those who make mistakes, does he hold this attitude at the expense of the integrity of doctrine? Should purity of doctrine prevail over love and acceptance for the sinner? By accepting the sinner, am I justifying my behavior and disavowing doctrine?

Certainly not, as we hope we have shown for specific cases in the previous pages. However, we can also note that the Pope himself sets the standard of interpretation and takes responsibility for the special sensitivity or anxiety of some pastors and does so through these words we have already quoted in the preceding pages:

> I understand those who prefer a more rigorous pastoral care which leaves no room for confusion. But I sincerely believe that Jesus wants a Church attentive to the goodness which the Holy Spirit sows in the midst of human weakness, a Mother who, while clearly expressing her objective teaching, "always does what good she can, even if in the process, her shoes get soiled by the mud of the street."[1] (#308)

This is another way of expressing the hermeneutic of the person.

For Pope Francis, this hermeneutic does not remain something merely theoretical, but translates into feelings of compassion and tenderness. The Pope often returns to this theme of special tenderness toward those who suffer.

And now I will not use my own words, but the words of Francis at the Sunday *Angelus* of February 15, 2015; it is a little gem. Here's what he said:

> In these Sundays, Mark the Evangelist speaks to us about Jesus' actions against every type of evil, for the benefit of those suffering in body and spirit: the possessed, the sick, sinners....In today's Gospel (cf.

Mark 1:40–45)…Jesus responds to this humble and trusting prayer because his soul is moved to deep pity: compassion. "Compassion" is a most profound word: compassion means "to suffer-with-another." Jesus' heart manifests God's paternal compassion for that man, moving close to him and touching him. And this detail is very important. Jesus "stretched out his hand and touched him….And immediately the leprosy left him, and he was made clean" (vv. 41–42)….The Gospel of the healing of the leper tells us today that, if we want to be true disciples of Jesus, we are called to become, united to Him, instruments of his merciful love, overcoming every kind of marginalization.

NOTES

1. *Evangelii Gaudium*, 45.

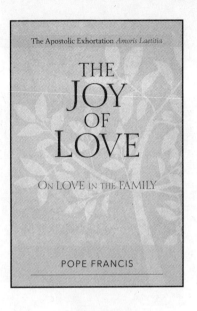

THE
JOY OF
LOVE

On Love in the Family;
The Apostolic Exhortation
Amoris Laetitia

Pope Francis

The Holy Father draws from the wisdom of Church teaching and dialogue from the recent synods to present a complete message on the most profound human community, the family.

978-0-8091-5318-3 $11.95

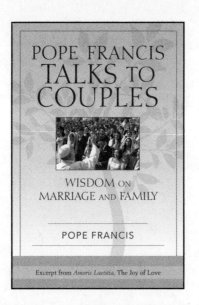

POPE FRANCIS TALKS TO COUPLES

Wisdom on Marriage and Family; Excerpt from *Amoris Laetitia, The Joy of Love*

Pope Francis

Pope Francis keeps a special place in his heart for married couples. These two chapters, drawn from his much larger letter, *The Joy of Love: On Love in the Family*, are dedicated to couples. Because he expressly suggests that couples read chapters four and five from *The Joy of Love*, they are now available in this volume. In many ways, it is his conversation with couples: those thinking about marriage, those newly married, those living their marriage.

978-0-8091-5325-1 _ $7.95